EW CR

## LEABHARLANNA CHONTAE NA GAILLIMHE
## (GALWAY COUNTY LIBRARIES)

Acc. No. 419,041        Class No. 821 OCO

| Date of Return | Date of Return | Date of Return |
|---|---|---|
|  |  |  |
|  |  |  |
|  |  |  |
|  |  |  |
|  |  |  |

Books are on loan for 21 days from date of issue.

Fines for overdue books: 10p for each week or portion of a week plus cost of postage incurred in recovery.

Patrick J. O'Connor

# *PEOPLE POWER PLACE*

Oireacht na Mumhan Books

Published in Ireland by
Oireacht na Mumhan Books
Coolanoran
Newcastle West
Co. Limerick

Printed by Litho Press Co.
Midleton, Co. Cork

821
OCO

L119.041
£8.00

# *Contents*

# *Figures*

# I

no
the sky
is not
bigger in Montana. When
for instance you come
from Williston
there seems at the border a change
but it is only because man has
built a tavern there.

- Ed Dorn, 'Idaho Out', in *Geography*,
London : Fulcrum Press, 1965.

# *Salt of the Earth*

Fathom it out
of a lake
amplitudinous as France
that bakes
like crazy pavement
beneath the fire of the sun.

On the high steppes
of the Andes
ever before Bolivar
set foot
on a continent
or Lot's wife
entered their cosmos
the Chipayas knew

Its incandescence
and made of it wayside
stations to serve their Gods
and currency
to keep body and soul
and the wolf from the door.

Raised on marshy canyons
the llama is their conduit
to the barterage
of the valleys.
Before the caravan sets off
one of the herd is sacrificed
to Pachamana
the goddess of the Earth.

Now everything is apt to be revised
in a world pressured from outside -
rites of initiation,
ways of getting and spending,
holistic modes of living.
The caravan trail diminishes.

# *On Misrepresenting Chief Seattle's Missive to the American President*

*for Sharon Zimmerman*

God made the world
one and indivisible
The red man followed
his example of holistic vision
and moral sensibility
preaching a confraternity
with everything aloof in the sky
or grounded upon the earth
the mother of all that moves
and gives life.
'How can you buy or sell the sky
or the warmth of the land?'
The idea never entered the immemorial mind
until casts and cultures clashed
and destiny took a hand
of erasure and re-invention.
Where are the buffalo?
Gone!
Where are the wild horses?
Tamed!
The ground of all our nesting?
Changed!
The end of right living
The beginning of all our ends!

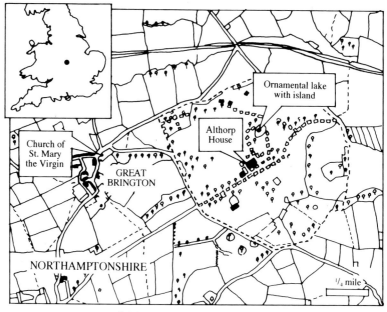

Althorp, Northamptonshire

# *Dianaland*

Within a bounded week
a place proclaimed itself
with investiture of a life
reposed under oak
planted by a mother
and her sons
within sight
of her childhood home.
She was Diana
Princess of Wales
and Spencer
was her name.
Ten made the bridge
to take her
to her grave
where her spirit
now presides,
and to catch
her world wide cult
the isle becomes her shrine.

# *Canine Commentary*

Once a dog fair was promised here.
That was long ago and far away,
and the dogs did not depart
                            for aeons.

Now as Mrs. Kelly puts it,
"the town's gone to the dogs:
there's nothing but young wans
                            wheelin' prams".

# Rí na Filí

*i.m. Michael Hartnett*

He took to himself
a necklace of wrens:
*muince dreoilíní*
for a life's work.

The elusive little bird
seeks a nest as pure and perfect
as the spirals round the universe:
a micro-cosmic rendering
of earth as home,
camouflaged, but clear,
to the king of all birds,
the king of all poets.

From the wren's nest
the poems come
nailed to the open air
in throaty clarion.

10

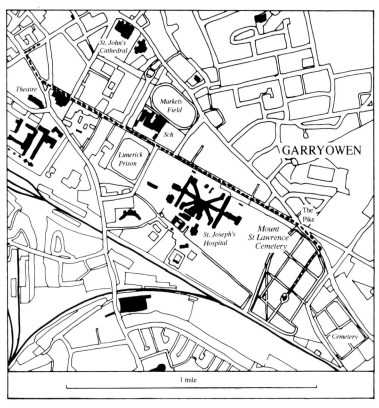

Slán le Jim Kemmy

# Cloch Beag ar a Charn

*i.m. Jim Kemmy*

The stuff that dreams are made on
Your life is rounded with a sleep
You took the mayoralty of your city
And made more of it than anyone before your time
You took the history of your city
And rendered a paper townscape
Voluminously for everyone who dares to care
A tithe as much as you    the gatherer
And the chronicler of people making places
Out of stone    and you a mason
With a heart as good as gold
Politician to the poor and the downtrodden
They all came to see you off
From Taoiseach to vagabond
Babes in arms    the sick    the infirm
The aged    the maimed
The well-heeled spectrum of society
Valediction for a true and combative spirit
Such a beautiful dreamer
Pure as snow upon a rose

*The title comes by way of a fetching phrase
from Gearóid Ó Tuathaigh in the course of
his graveside oration. Loosely translated, it
may pass as 'a small tribute'. In its Irish form,
it is redolent of the world of a stonemason.*

# *Clean Away*

The most exquisite sliver
of a golden flower
not known by any name
to me
came adrift
from the wreaths
on my mother's grave
and signalled her own
exquisite handiwork
a floral lampshade
made out of used nylons
dyed and worked into
a consummate show winner
all for the love
of the golden gift of hands

# II

Give me a place to stand, and I will move the world.

- Archimedes

# *Key to the Shells*

Three years of questing
for a transcendental geometry
to mirror a phantasmagoria
of wave and sail
as carapace
the great Dane arrived
at a raft
full of ellipses.

He sought and found
perfect harmony
between all the shapes
of a fantastic nautilus
and gave a ceramic
wonder to the world.

16

# *Winner Take All*

The Perch Meehan
trawls for flat fish
in a flat-bottomed lake.
'The perch', he says,
'is a clane fish!
He wouldn't live
in a cut-away!'
In suites of snipe-grass
the Perch makes a match
between Sonny whose father
went down in the Titanic
before the gosson was born
and Sissy, the daughter of Kate.
Between three women
and a man,
life is askew.
On the day of the thatching
the thatcher gets the full breast
and the gosson the wing
of a chicken.
Sonny nudges the breast
of a black woman
in wild imaginings.
Perch comes with one hand
as long as the other
on land and on water.

# *A Minute's Silence*

On departing the waffle station
in the Forum Hotel Cracow
A motor mouth of an American
is pitching in at the self-service counter.

He is momentarily stunned
trying to spike
an obstinate piece of Polish
to say cheese.

## *Viva Voce*

Trains forestalled?
Nothing for it
but to rise with the birds
and see the columns of mist
oscillate over the heads of yearlings
camped by lone thorn trees at Reens
and boot it through the morning
quietude to within a cuckoo-spit of Dublin
and the snare of the Red Cow
when news of the inter-city trains
breaks through. The word is bad.
At the head of the Coombe
a dog waits, the traffic abates,
he looks right, then left,
and crosses the road
at his own private pedestrian crossing.
We reach the portals
and the cobblestones
consult the noticeboard
and find.

# *Making Place*

Minor miracles are local
and so are resurrections.
Lazarus and the Lord
appeared in swaddling
not to the many
but the few.
They made the place
news to be retailed
across the wavelengths
            of the world.

20

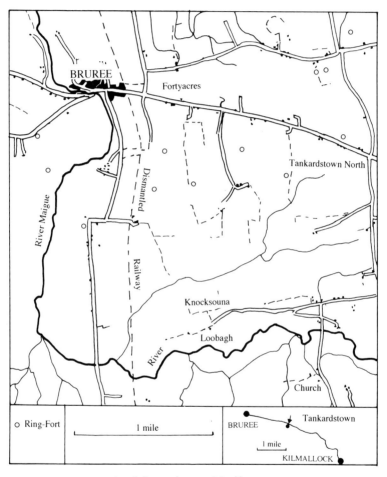

An Mangaire sa bhaile

# *An Mangaire*

To establish his identity
take off the Joycean mask
and find the three crowns of Munster
studded in his visage.
Find him at ease across
the green and white of Limerick
and the gold of Ireland.
Find him on peregrination in distant lands
before the days of massed touristic forays.
Find him as columnist of the *Leader*
these five and fifty years
distilling the ambient mood
of a kind and gentle spirit
for all to overhear and read
on ......... to the millennium.
Find him in Kilfinane
the gatherer of a gathering
making a bridge to a Joycean past
pulling identity and memory together.
Find him on the borderland
of parishes all written up
at home in Tankardstown
with *céad fáilte* for a greeting
and a smile at open door.

22 April 1999

# *P to the Power of*

Death came to me once
of a grey January
outside my old home
hooded and cloaked
death came to me
flighted and flown
blown upon my countenance
sown inside my head with psychic thread
and my heart went out
to the winged messenger.

# *Leopard in Tree*

Passing by on the busy road
that skirts Nairobi National Park
a clear-sighted bus driver
picked from the middle-distance
foliage a leopard embossed and still
part of the tapestry of the trees.

Seldom seen even on safari
this shy and declining animal
was there on the way back
and stirred to vindicate the vision.
Was it perspicacity
pure and driven?
or did the leopard
habituate the tree?

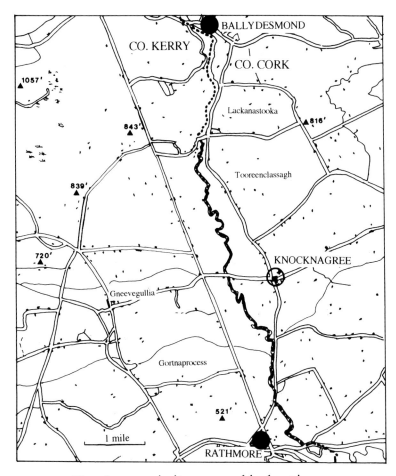

Knocknagree in its geographical setting

# *Knocknagree Fair Glossary*

Bird and plant
find their own vernacular
in the vendors' hill domain -
*naosc, gall-luachair, aitinn Gaelach,*
and the habitats where these lay down -
*móinteán, gleanntán, puiteach.*
In the last best west
lone animals of the field
translate into truculent
battlers on the road
with *nasc, púicín* and *adhastar,*
from Gneevegullia and Gortnaprocess,
Tooreenclassagh and Lackanastooka.
Coteries of O'Keeffes, Kellehers, Flemings,
Dennehys, Moynihans, McCarthys,
two and thirty other long-tailed clans
and stragglers by the running score,
with cattle, sheep and pigs converge
on a green fit
for a fabled stud of horses:
the hearth of Knocknagree,
where the houses melt back
from the *gleo* of the dancing tangler,
the *caimiléireacht* of the slithery chancer.

# *Dawn in Calvary*

Above the horizontal realm
in indeterminate light
the call-up of footfall
elicits flurries of inter-changeability,
but always keeping the ratio
of one crow to one headstone.
Big-beaked, smug, otherwordly,
they treat the cemetery
with the proprietorial air
of home.

# III

Give me a map: then let me see how much
Is left for me to conquer all the world, ----
Cutting the tropic line of Capricorn,
I conquered all as far as Zanzibar.

- Christopher Marlowe, *Tamburlaine*, Part II
(V. iii. 123-39)

# *Guides to Exotic Townlands*

(1-36 in alphabetical order. Each quatrain is preceded by county
of origin and the relevant Ordnance Survey 1:10,560 sheet(s) )

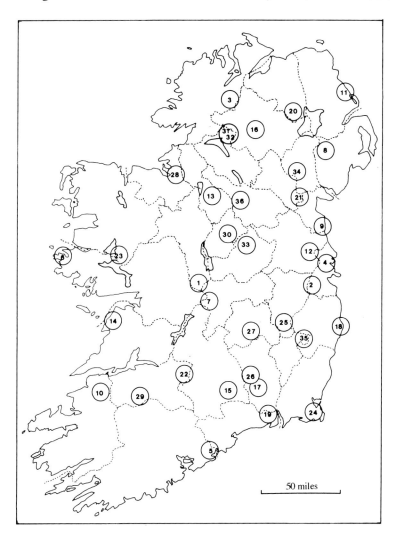

50 miles

# America

1 (Roscommon 54, 56)

Quare genius gave the warrant
To the land of the free
And the home of the brave
Upon the plains of Connacht.

# Banshee

2 (Dublin 20)

Wailing, weeping
Soughing, whispering
Only once presaged death
and place christening.

# Blackrepentance

3 (Donegal 69)

Dry, unleavened bread,
Black tea, rounds, rosaries
Fail to give the edge over
St. Patrick's Purgatory, Lough Derg.

# *Brazil*

**4** (Dublin 11)

Greeting to our friends,
The *mestizos* and *mullattos*
On the doorstep of Dublin,
Where the Sao Francisco flows.

# *Cock-and-the-Bull*

**5** (Cork 67)

In this place of tall tales
One story is good; another is told:
Skyscrapers are *not* the last word,
Unless felled by a swirl in the ashes.

# *Courhoor*

**6** (Galway 22)

In a week of Sundays,
It's the closest call
Or slightest slip of the tongue
To the core of cutehoordom.

# *Cuba*

**7** (King's Co. 21,29)

A Hispanic island
In the Faithful County:
Guevara, Marti, Castro -
Revolutionaries abroad in Offaly.

# *Edenordinary*

**8** (Down 27)

God created man
And woman, and gave
Them Edenic pleasure,
Reduced after the Fall.

# *Ganderstown*

**9** (Louth 22)

The male of the best flock
In the *vill* puts himself
In the way of drink
And enduring notoriety.

# *Garryantanvally*

**10** (Kerry 10, 16, 17)


A dog's dinner of a rendering
For a garden long husbanded:
The English transliterators
Went to town on old Ireland.


# *Greenland*

**11** (Antrim 35, 40)


The writing's in the sky
As the geese fly over:
Home letters mutate
In their formation.


# *Jealoustown*

**12** (Meath 38)


Jealousy comes
In the colour of jade:
A family gives name to a place
Sub-infeudated, stolid and staid.

34

# Keshcarrigan

**13** (Leitrim 24, 28)


'The wickerwork causeway
Of the little rock':
Surely not! *Kesh* is clannish,
And well begot.


# Lisdoonvarna

**14** (Clare 8)


*Lios* and *dún* may be synonymous,
The waters good for a double christening:
Then there's a gap
Of the wildest imagining.


# Madamsland

**15** (Tipperary 70)


*Madame* in county Cork
Sends a message
By *Horse and Jockey*
To her estate in Tipp.

# Meetinghouse-hill

**16** (Tyrone 35)

Without pretence of church
Or chapel, the word of the preacher
Spreads and finds a simple node
To impart a simple message.

# Memory

**17** (Kilkenny 31)

The remembrance of things past
Within intimate, defiant space
May be our most striking link
To another time, another place.

# Merrymeeting

**18** Wicklow 25)

The *raparees*
Come down
From the hills
To party.

# Mountmisery

**19** (Waterford 9)

Whenever the eponymous owner
Scaled the heights,
He left behind
A long string

# Moymucklemurry

**20** (Derry 46)

A sweet, alliterative
flow through the Derry air,
Or pigs upon a plain
With a swineherd.

# Mucker

**21** (Monaghan 29, 32)

Paddy Kavanagh's cradle
Once abounded in pigs:
The place was born to rhyme
And the poet to suffer.

# *Nicker*

**22** (Limerick 24)

Elide an element,
And it's not the singular
Of what comes in a pair.
Behold! it's a rabbit resort.

# *Nymphsfield*

**23** (Mayo 120)

Blond, nubile girls
Dance in a western field,
Climb the pillars of the sun,
And then as suddenly, disappear.

# *Paradise*

**24** (Wexford 47)

Once promised *in extremis*,
It made a protracted journeying,
Resisted all blandishments,
And took hold in the Model County.

38

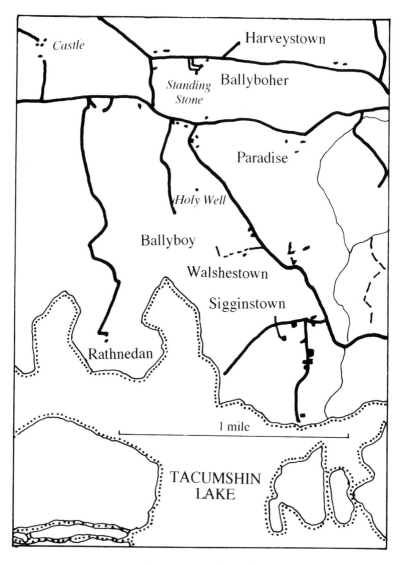

Gateway to Paradise

# Paudeenourstown

**25** (Kildare 35)

The claimant
To the English *town*
Is an unmistakable
Gael, and clansman.

# Physicianstown

**26** (Kilkenny 26)

A healing place
Where O'Malley, the painter,
Celebrates little things
And casts an inner eye.

# Poormansbridge

**27** (Queen's Co. 23)

Place of parting, loss,
atrophy, anomie,
Droichead na Deor,
Briseadh Chroí.

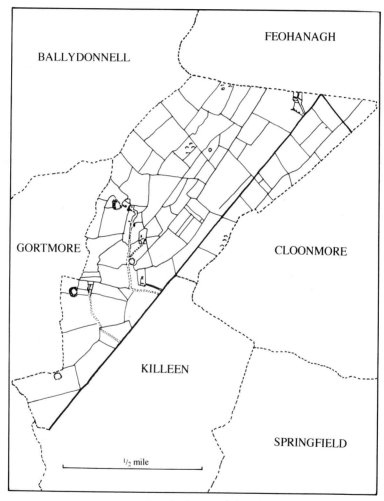

Rathpalatine in its townland setting

# *Primrosegrange*

**28** (Sligo 14, 20)

Smiles are banked
On monastic land,
And the flowers
Re-appear every spring.

# *Rathpalatine*

**29** (Limerick 45)

In 1720 John Jost Koning
Lived on the Copley estate,
And left an exotic suffix,
To compound with the townland of *Ráth*.

# *Rhine*

**30** (Longford 9)

Contemplate the scale of transfer
Out of Germany
To a place near *France*
In Longford.

42

## Rotten Mountain

**31** (Fermanagh 1, 2)


Someone did the dirty
To the denizens
Of a place that never
Reeked of putrefaction.


## Sheemuldoon

**32** (Fermanagh 6)


The Professor of Poetry at Oxford
Thralls through a paper mountain,
And finds his chair
Suspended in otherworldliness.


## Soho

**33** (Westmeath 6)


Red lights,
Blue movies,
Purple patches,
In Lakeland.

# *Tievenamara*

**34** (Armagh 20, 23, 24)

To catch the edge of the sea
On the Monaghan-Armagh borderland,
Is an exquisite exercise
In failure to touch.

# *Vermont*

**35** (Carlow 4, 9)

*Newengland*
In Kilkenny:
A touch of it
In Carlow.

# *Yewer*

**36** Cavan 19)

The tree
Of afterlife
Is evergreen,
And poisonous.

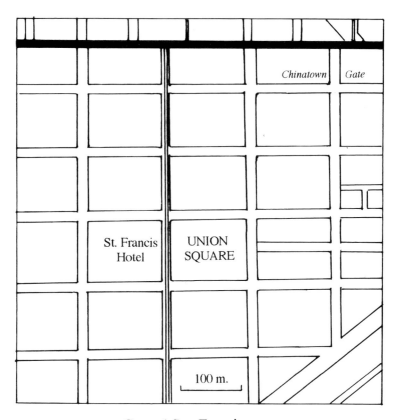

Central San Francisco

# *San Francisco : July Night*

*for Cathal Ó Searcaigh*

Skyscrapers misted like mountain tops
Alcatraz an unseen sentinel flashing
                                    on and off
a blast in the wind that would cut through
the spillage of mental hospitals onto streets
a taxi cruising past the St. Francis
on Union Square   windows rolled down
Glenn Miller's alter ego   *in the mood*
to catch the cool night air
beggars at every corner
a hatcha gotcha placarded weirdo world
tied like snails to shells
in the city by the bay.
Where's the scatter of gold?
the Beat Generation?
the power of petals?
life by technicolor flags?
Movers and shakers living by the dollar
indigents choking on their own vomit.
The silent voice settles nothing.

46

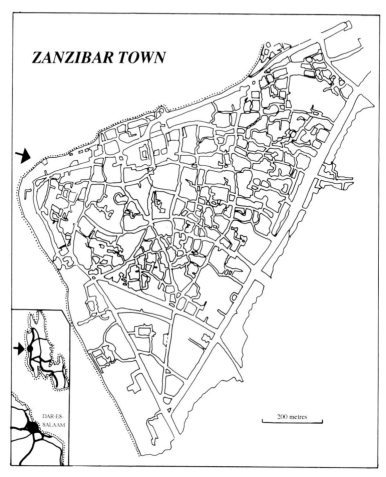

ZANZIBAR TOWN

DAR-ES-
SALAAM

200 metres

Warren of Zanzibar (Stonetown)

# *Zanzibar Nocturnal*

Hassan sent by Mercury
leads us a gay fandango
through the warren at dusk.

Round every corner
it opens like a chapter
from the Book of Revelations:
Galileo somnambulating across turrets
and minarets, fixing upon stars,
in a star-struck sky:
Beelzebub sitting in an alleyway
flooded by the light of the moon
re-embroidering a map of the fires of damnation:
the Bohemian girl in an alcove
combing her hair by brazier-light
rhapsodied, then ravished, by the hellish infidel:
conspiratorial voices in a backlane
all talk of Bismillah as imperative to sunder
and proclaim a cradled domain upon the waves:
Scaramouch of the loud mouth and vacant mind
butts in and eggs them on
to the brink of a verbal revolution.

A whole concatenation of events
dances round this place
and nowhere else.

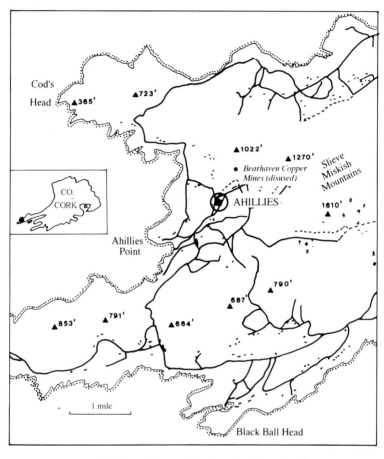

Ahillies, Beara Peninsula, Co. Cork

# *Allihies*

There's a mustard church
to cohere a village
and embolden the colours
of extremity.
Around the village
folios of fields
are patterned green:
one on an outreach
is taken from the mouth
of a fecund wilderness.
Striations make bold on rock
like organ pipes
that heather dares to climb:
abandoned cars, abandoned copper mines.
The shafts this winter's day
are of Sol's trajectory
casting light and shadow
on green and rocky hills
and dormancy dusted down or golden.
The reach of land
and sea casts no such edge.
Gulls and cormorants go out to feed:
a horse grazes a diminutive field
held by fuchsia in seasonal amend:
peace over all the land,
peace at land's end.

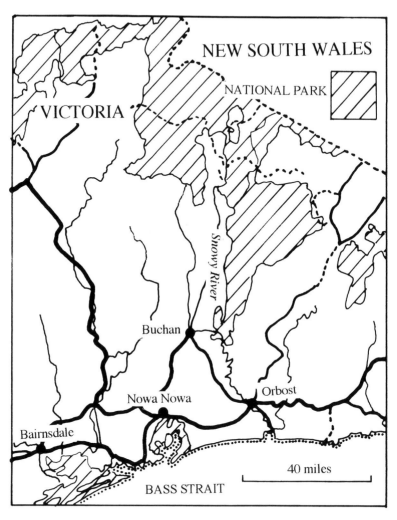

Buchan, East Gippsland, Victoria

# *Buchan*

Wombats of a sluggish night move
lie corpsed along the road from Nowa Nowa
towards a place sans corner boys
to rhyme the name obscenely.
This idyllic gateway to the Snowy.
Green village in verdant valley
of set pieces in an edging
single specimens all to wrest fragility
from out of the maw of the wild.
Bearded man and matronly woman
step out of the Bush or the Bible
a ute[1] and kelpie clientele stand surrogate.
The school bus still not done
turns at dusk.
A wan new moon settles nocturnals.
At dawn the saw factory
sends up smoke
in a plume or awning
to dent bucolic images of Arcadia
and the young go early
from the homesteads stitched
into the green quilt of the valley.
Hazard and handicap
in one sweet spot
slowly turning over
upon the face of the earth.

1. Utility vehicle or pick-up truck

# *Power of Place*

A place without words
is a place where nothing
happens, that dissolves
into the soup of space.

*Ab urbe condita*
to a mountain
of words,
Rome becomes.

Places are
called up,
written in,
talked over,
revised,
re-written,
re-visited,
with words.